The First Dragon Riddle Book

Also by Joseph Rosenbloom

The Second Dragon Riddle Book

Joseph Rosenbloom

The First Dragon
Riddle Book

Illustrated by Joyce Behr

DRAGON
GRANADA PUBLISHING
London Toronto Sydney New York

This abridged edition published by
Granada Publishing Limited in Dragon Books 1978
Reprinted 1979

ISBN 0 583 30265 3

First published by Sterling Publishing Co Inc 1976
as *The Biggest Riddle Book in the World*
Copyright © Joseph Rosenbloom 1976

Granada Publishing Limited
Frogmore, St Albans, Herts AL2 2NF
and
3 Upper James Street, London W1R 4BP
866 United Nations Plaza, New York, NY 10017, USA
117 York Street, Sydney, NSW 2000, Australia
100 Skyway Avenue, Rexdale, Ontario, M9W 3A6 Canada
PO Box 84165, Greenside, 2034, Johannesburg, South Africa
CML Centre, Queen & Wyndham, Auckland 1, New Zealand

Made and printed in Great Britain by
Richard Clay (The Chaucer Press) Ltd
Bungay, Suffolk
Set in Linotype Times

Granada ®
Granada Publishing ®

To:
Michelle, Michael and Eric

Contents

1 Warm Ups

What happens when you throw a green rock in the Red Sea?

It gets wet.

What does an envelope say when you lick it?

Nothing. It just shuts up.

Why shouldn't you tell a secret to a pig?

Because he is a squealer.

Where do frogs sit?

On toadstools.

Why should you leave your watch at home when you take an aeroplane?

Because time flies anyway.

If a man were born in Greece, raised in Spain, went to America, and died in San Francisco, what is he?

Dead.

How can you tell twin witches apart?

It's not easy to tell witch is which.

What weighs more: a pound of lead or a pound of feathers?

They weigh the same.

Why do people always say to you, 'A penny for your thoughts'?

Because that's all they are worth.

7

What doesn't get any wetter no matter how much it rains?

The ocean.

Why did the man have to fix the horn of his car?

Because it didn't give a hoot.

Why did the nutty kid throw a bucket of water out of the window?

He wanted to make a big splash.

Why did the nutty kid throw butter out of the window?

He wanted to see a butterfly.

Why did the nutty kid throw a glass of water out of the window?

He wanted to see a waterfall.

What can you break without touching it?

Your promise.

A man was driving a black truck. His lights were not on. The moon was not out. A lady was crossing the street. How did the man see her?

It was a bright, sunny day.

What animal makes the most of its food?

The giraffe. It makes a little go a long way.

What insect gets A's in English?

    A spelling bee.

When a dirty kid has finished taking a bath, what is still dirty?

    The bathtub.

What kind of bath can you take without water?

    A sun bath.

What time is the same spelled backward or forward?

    Noon.

What do you get if you cross an insect and a rabbit?

    Bugs Bunny.

Why can't you read a story about a bed?

    It hasn't been made up yet.

Why did the kid avoid the cemetery?

    He wouldn't be caught dead there.

What did the bee say to the flower?

    'Hello, honey!'

What did the fly say to the flypaper?

    'I'm stuck on you.'

What did the tree say to the woodpecker?

    'You bore me.'

What colour was Napoleon's white horse?

    White.

Why did the kid put his clock in the oven?

    He wanted to have a hot time.

If you want to get rich, why should you keep your mouth shut?

    Because silence is golden.

What is drawn by everyone without pen or pencil?
Breath.

What goes around a yard but doesn't move?
A fence.

Why does a mother carry her baby?
The baby can't carry the mother.

What is a calf after it is six months old?
Seven months old.

What asks no question but demands an answer?
A doorbell or a ringing telephone.

What kind of apple has a short temper?
A crab apple.

How does a boat show affection?
It hugs the shore.

What kind of watch is best for people who don't like time on their hands?
A pocket watch.

What goes up and down but doesn't move?
A staircase.

What always comes into a house through the keyhole?
A key.

What word if pronounced right is wrong but if pronounced wrong is right?

Wrong.

What song does a car radio play?

A cartoon (car tune).

What has four legs and a back but no body?

A chair.

When does a chair dislike you?

When it can't bear you.

How did the man feel when he got a big bill from the electric company?

He was shocked.

What did the man do when he got a big gas bill?

He exploded.

What did the man say when he got a big phone bill?

'Who said talk is cheap?'

What is the best day to go to the beach?

Sunday.

What kind of bulbs don't need water?

Light bulbs.

Why is a fish like a person who talks too much?

Because it doesn't know when to keep its mouth shut.

How can you tell the difference between a can of chicken soup and a can of tomato soup?

Read the label.

What trees come in twos?

Pear (pair) trees.

What insect runs away from everything?

A flea (flee).

2 Quickies

What kind of money do monsters use?
   Weirdo (weird dough).

Why did the window pane blush?
   It saw the weather-strip.

When is the moon heaviest?
   When it is full.

How do you file a nail?
   Under the letter N.

What is a parrot?
   A wordy birdy.

What fly has laryngitis?
   A horsefly (hoarse fly).

Why did the kid keep his shirt on when he took a bath?
   Because the label said 'Wash and Wear.'

What kind of water can't freeze?
   Hot water.

What did the big watch hand say to the small hand?
   'Got a minute?'

What did one broom say to the other broom?
   'Have you heard the latest dirt?

What did the electric plug say to the wall?
   'Socket to me!'

Why is an old car like a baby playing?
Because it goes with a rattle.

What knights rode camels?
The Arabian Nights (knights).

What is Dracula's favourite sport?
Bat-minton (badminton).

What letter is like a vegetable?
The letter P.

Why do people work as bakers?
Because they knead (need) the dough.

What is a sleeping bag?
A knapsack (nap sack).

Where do ants go when they want to eat?
To a restaur-ant.

What is the opposite of restaurant?
Workerant.

Who has friends for lunch?
A cannibal.

What time is it when a clock strikes thirteen?
Time to get it fixed.

What is the most valuable fish?
Goldfish.

What is a ghost's favourite rock?
Tombstone.

When is a man like a dog?
When he is a boxer.

What do you call a greasy chicken?
A slick chick.

Why did the cowboy ride his horse?
Because the horse was too heavy to carry.

Can you spell eighty in two letters?
A-T.

Why are nappies like £5 notes?
Because you have to change them.

Which end of a bus is it best to get off?
It doesn't matter. Both ends stop.

How does a fireplace feel?
Grate! (Great!)

What did Napoleon become after his 39th year?
40 years old.

What cat lives in the ocean?
An octopus.

What would you call a beautiful cat?
A glamour puss.

What do you get if you feed a lemon to your cat?
A sourpuss.

What kind of lock is on a hippie's door?
A padlock.

Why did the man put a clock under his desk?
He wanted to work overtime.

What is a very hard subject?
The study of rocks.

Why was the boy's suit rusty?
It was guaranteed to wear like iron.

What stays hot in the refrigerator?
Mustard.

What kind of key opens a coffin?
A skeleton key.

What is a broken-down hot rod?
A shot rod.

Why is the moon like a dollar?
It has four quarters.

Why are rivers lazy?
Because they never get off their beds.

When is a chair like a fabric?
When it is sat in (satin).

Why was the horse all charged up?
Because it ate haywire.

What is ice?
Skid stuff.

What sea creature can add?
An octoplus.

What is a vampire's favourite soup?
Alpha-bat (alphabet) soup.

What is bought by the yard and worn by the foot?
A carpet.

What have eyes but can't see?
Needles, storms and potatoes.

Why did the ocean roar?
Because it had crabs in its bed.

What insect can be spelled with just one letter?
Bee.

Why did Batman go to the pet shop?
To buy a Robin.

3 Ask Your Friends
—If You Dare!

What is a forum?

Two-um plus two-um.

How do mountains hear?

With mountaineers.

Spell Indian tent with two letters.

TP.

What is the proverb about catching a cold?

'Win a flu (few), lose a flu.'

What happened to the wolf who fell into the washing machine?

He became a wash and werewolf.

When is it difficult to get your watch off your wrist?

When it's ticking (sticking) there.

Why is a mouse like hay?

Because the cat'll (cattle) eat it.

Why doesn't Sweden export cattle?

Because she wants to keep her Stockholm (stock home).

How many peas are there in a pint?

There is only one P in 'pint.'

Why is a barefoot boy like an Eskimo?

The barefoot boy wears no shoes and the Eskimo wears snowshoes.

At what time do most people go to the dentist?

At tooth-hurty (2:30).

Why is Saturday night important to Julius's girl friend?

That's when Julius Caesar (sees her).

How much is 5Q and 5Q?

'10Q.'
'You're welcome.'

Can you spell soft and slow with two letters?

EZ.

What would happen if everyone in the country bought a pink car?

We would have a pink carnation (car nation).

Where do you end up if you smoke too much?

Coffin (coughin').

What is the best way to send a letter to the Easter Bunny?

By hare (air) mail.

When someone comes to your door, what is the polite thing to do?

Vitamin (invite him in).

Can you spell a composition with two letters?

SA (essay).

When is a grown man still a child?

When he is a miner (minor).

Where were the first French fries made?

In Greece (grease).

Why do ships use knots instead of miles?

To keep the sea tide (tied).

What vegetable is dangerous to have aboard ship?

A leek (leak).

What did the boy gopher say to the girl gopher?

'I gopher (go for) you.'

What did the boy firefly say to the girl firefly?

'I glow for you.'

What did the boy banana say to the girl banana?

'You have a lot of appeal.'

How can you spell rot with two letters?

DK (decay).

If you add 2-forget and 2-forget, what do you get?

4-gotten.

What did Delaware?

She wore her New Jersey.

Why did the lady hold her ears when she passed the chickens?

Because she didn't want to hear their foul (fowl) language.

What musical instrument from Spain helps you fish?

A cast-a-net (castanet).

What is the difference between a fish and a piano?

You can't tuna fish.

If you put three ducks in a carton, what do you get?

A box of quackers.

What girl's name is like a letter?

Kay (K).

What has four wheels and flies?

A dustbin lorry.

What did one tooth say to the other tooth?

'Thar's gold in them thar fills.'

What is the first thing ghosts do when they get into a car?

They fasten their sheet (seat) belts.

What do you call a boy named Lee whom no one wants to talk to?

Lonely (Lone-Lee).

When did the fly fly?

When the spider spied her.

A man and a dog were going down the street. The man rode, yet walked. What was the dog's name?

Yet.

Why do windows squeak when you open them?

Because they have panes (pains).

Why is a shirt with 8 buttons so interesting?

Because you fascinate (fasten 8).

When is a letter damp?

When it has postage due (dew).

Why is Ireland so rich?

Because its capital is always Dublin (doublin').

How can you prove that a horse has six legs?

A horse has four legs (forelegs) in front and two behind.

What did the jack say to the car?

'Can I give you a lift?'

What do you call your mother's other sister?

Deodorant (the other aunt).

Where does the sandman keep his sleeping sand?

In his knapsack (nap sack).

4 Sick!

When is the vet busiest?
When it rains cats and dogs.

When don't you feel so hot?
When you catch a cold.

What means of transportation gives people colds?
A choo-choo train.

What is the difference between a bus driver and a cold?
One knows the stops, the other stops the nose.

Why does a dentist seem moody?
Because he always looks down in the mouth.

What would you call a small wound?
A short cut.

Which eye gets hit the most?
A bullseye.

When a girl slips on the ice, why can't her brother help her up?
He can't be a brother and assist her (a sister) too.

What kind of television programme tells you who just broke an arm or leg?
A newscast.

How can you tell if a mummy has a cold?
He stars coffin (coughin')

25

What is the difference between a hill and a pill?

A hill is hard to get up, a pill is hard to get down.

What is the famous last word in surgery?

'Ouch!'

Why did the germ cross the microscope?

To get to the other side.

What sickness do cowboys get from riding wild horses?

Bronchitis (bronc-itis).

Why did the fireplace call the doctor?

Because the chimney had the flu (flue).

Why do your eyes look different when you come from an eye doctor?

Because they've been checked.

Why is a pony like a person with a sore throat?

Because they are both a little hoarse (horse).

Why did the doctor give up his practice?

Because he lost his patience (patients).

How do you make a thin person fat?

Throw him up in the air and he comes down 'plump.'

What do you get if an axe hits your head?

A splitting headache.

When they take out an appendix, it's an appendectomy; when they remove your tonsils, it's a tonsillectomy. What is it when they remove a growth from your head?

A haircut.

How did the clock feel when no one wound it up?

Run down.

How can you keep from getting a sharp pain in your eye when you drink chocolate milk?

Take the spoon out of the glass.

What is a sick crocodile?

An illigator.

Why did the secretary cut her fingers off?

She wanted to write shorthand.

If you don't feel well, what do you probably have?

A pair of gloves on your hands.

What is the difference between a boxer and a man with a cold?

A boxer knows his blows, a man with a cold blows his nose.

If you fell off a ladder, what would you fall against?

Against your will.

What do you get if you put your head in a washing machine?

Cleaner and brighter thoughts.

When is the best time to buy a thermometer?

In the winter, because then it is lower.

What is the best thing to take when you're run over?

The number of the car that hit you.

Why was the chicken sick?

It had people pox.

What is better than presence of mind in an automobile accident?

Absence of body.

What did the doctor say to the tonsil?

'You look so cute, I think I'll take you out.'

What has fifty legs but can't walk?

Half a centipede.

What is worse than a centipede with sore feet?

A giraffe with a sore throat.

What is worse than a giraffe with a sore throat?

A turtle with claustrophobia.

What is worse than a turtle with claustrophobia?

An elephant with hay fever.

Why shouldn't you make jokes about a fat person?

Because it's not nice to poke fun at someone else's expanse (expense).

What do seven days of dieting do?

They make one weak (week).

What is the best way to lose weight?

Learn to play the piano, and you can pound away all you want.

You never catch cold going up in a lift. True or false?

True. You come down with a cold, never up.

If an apple a day keeps the doctor away, what will an onion do?

Keep everyone away.

Where do squirrels go when they have nervous breakdowns?

To the nut house.

What kind of animal needs oiling?

A mouse. It squeaks.

What happens when a pony gets sunburned?

You get a little horseradish (reddish).

Why did the farmer take the cow to the vet?

Because she was so moo-dy.

What do you have if your head is hot, your feet are cold, and you see spots in front of your eyes?

You probably have a polka-dotted sock over your head.

What did Frankenstein say when a bolt of lightning hit him?

'Thanks, I needed that!'

When do you have acute pain?

When you own a very pretty window.

How did the bread feel when it was put in the toaster?

It was burned up.

5 Goodies & Baddies

Who supervises children when they play games?

The game warden.

What criminal doesn't take baths?

A dirty crook.

Why do surgeons wear masks during operations?

Because if they make a mistake, no one will know who did it.

What insect is religious?

A praying mantis.

What dog is religious?

A prairie dog.

Why did the man hit the clock?

Because the clock struck first.

What did the big toe say to the little toe?

'There's a big heel following us.'

How do you make an eggroll (egg roll)?

Push it.

Did you hear the story about the burp?

Never mind. It's not worth repeating.

What kind of music does a ghost like?

Haunting melodies.

Why is it dangerous to do maths in the jungle?

If you add 4 and 4 you get 8.

If you want to learn how to fight, what book should you read?

A scrapbook.

What is yellow and wears a mask?

The Lone Lemon.

What is a pie in the sky?

A flying pizza.

What did the mother elephant say to the baby elephant when it misbehaved?

'*Tusk, tusk!*'

Why did the farmer plant sugar cubes?

Because he wanted to raise cane.

What kind of long-distance calls do ministers make when they speak to each other?

Parson-to-parson (person-to-person).

If you cross a bee and chopped meat, what do you get?

A humburger.

Why did the orchestra have bad manners?

Because it didn't know how to conduct itself.

Why is mayonnaise never ready?

Because it is always dressing.

What did the banana do when the monkey chased it?

The banana split.

Why did the jelly roll?

Because it saw the apple turnover.

What kind of cake should you serve to chicken?

Layer cake.

What kind of eggs does a wicked chicken lay?

Devilled eggs.

What did the chicken say when it was put in the pot?

'*Boy, am I in hot water!*'

What hired killer never goes to jail?

The exterminator.

How do you make a Mexican chili?

Take him to the North Pole.

Why is a robber strong?

Because he holds people up.

Why was the invisible mother upset with her invisible child?

Because he was always appearing.

What is a prizefighter's favourite drink?

Punch.

Which hand should you use to stir tea?

Neither. It is better to use a spoon.

How can you tell if there is an elephant sleeping in your bed?

Look for peanut shells.

How can you keep a barking dog quiet?

With hush puppies.

What is small, purple and dangerous?

A grape with a machine gun.

What do you get when two strawberries meet?

A strawberry shake.

Why are Egyptian children good children?

Because they respect their mummies.

What is a hippie mummy?

A deady-o.

Where do tough chickens come from?

From hard-boiled eggs.

What did the father mummy say to the kid mummy when he asked for a sweet?

'You had some a century ago!'

How do you know if a drink is any good?

A little swallow tells you.

What cruel person would sit on a baby?

A baby sitter.

What gun does a police dog use?

A dogmatic.

What is a policeman's favourite snack?

Copcakes (*cupcakes*).

Who is Count Dracula's favourite person on a baseball team?

The bat boy.

6 Fooling Mother Nature

Why was the mother flea so sad?

Because her children were going to the dogs.

What do you call nervous insects?

Jitterbugs.

What do people do in China when it rains?

Let it rain.

What is a dimple?

A pimple going the other way.

What is black and yellow and goes zzub, zzub?

A bee going backwards.

What is the snappiest snake?

A garter snake.

Why are cards like wolves?

Because they belong to a pack.

What do you get if you cross a worm and a fur coat?

A caterpillar.

What do you get if you cross a skunk and a bee?

An animal that stinks as it stings.

Why do the hippies study the stars?

Because they are so far out.

If an electric train travels 90 miles an hour in a westerly direction and the wind is blowing from the north, in which direction is the smoke blowing?

There is no smoke from an electric train!

What do you get if you cross a kangaroo and a raccoon?

A fur coat with pockets.

What insect is like the top of a house?

A tick (attic).

What is a foreign ant?

Important.

Why are spiders like tops?

Because they are always spinning.

When does a female deer need money?

When she doesn't have a buck.

What is the difference between a train and a teacher?

A train goes 'Choo-choo', but a teacher tells you to take the gum out of your mouth.

Why didn't the man believe what the sardine said?

It sounded too fishy.

Why are mosquitoes annoying?

Because they get under your skin.

Why do flies walk on the ceiling?

If they walked on the floor, someone might step on them.

What did the dirt say to the rain?

'If this keeps up, my name will be mud.'

What kind of leopard has red spots?

A leopard with measles.

Where do black birds drink?

At a crowbar.

What is an easy way to make your money bigger?

Put it under a magnifying glass.

Why is the letter 'A' like a flower?

Because a bee comes after it.

If we breathe oxygen in the daytime, what do we breathe at night?

Nitrogen.

Why did the nature lover plant bird seed?

He wanted to grow canaries.

Why did the farmer plant old car parts in his garden?

He wanted to raise a bumper crop.

If a farmer raises wheat in dry weather, what does he raise in wet weather?

An umbrella.

What is a hot and noisy duck?

A firequacker.

What do you always leave behind because they are dirty?

Your footprints.

Why is a rabbit's nose always shiny?

Because his powder puff is on the wrong end.

What is the difference between an oak tree and a tight shoe?

One makes acorns, the other makes corns ache.

Why should you never tell secrets in a garden?

Because the corn has ears, the potatoes have eyes, and the beans talk.

What is the best way to raise strawberries?

With a spoon.

Why is a garden like a story?

They both have plots.

Why do gardener's hate weeds?

Give weeds an inch and they'll take a yard.

If there were ten cats in a boat and one jumped out, how many would be left?

None, because they were all copycats.

What kind of person is fed up with people?

A cannibal.

If a rooster laid a brown egg and a white egg, what kind of chicks would hatch?

None. Roosters don't lay eggs.

How can you eat an egg without breaking its shell?

Ask someone else to break it.

What did the tree say to the axe?

'I'm stumped.'

When can't astronauts land on the moon?

When it is full.

What is a ticklish subject?

The study of feathers.

What is the dirtiest word in the world?

Pollution.

How can a leopard change his spots?

Move to another place.

Why does a baby duck walk softly?

Because it is a baby and it can't walk, hardly.

When you take away two letters from this five-letter word, you get one. What word is it?

Stone.

What helps keep your teeth together.

Toothpaste.

Why are country people cleverer than city people?

Because the population is denser in big cities.

What kind of fish performs operations?

A sturgeon (surgeon).

In what way are the letter 'A' and noon the same?

Both are in the middle of day.

Why is it so wet in Great Britain?

Because of all the kings and queens that reigned there.

What bunch of animals can always be heard?

Cattle, because they go around in herds.

Why shouldn't you cry if your cow falls off a mountain?

There's no use in crying over spilt milk.

'Did you hear the story about the peacock?'

'It's a beautiful tail (tale).'

7 World Records

What is the biggest ant?

An elephant.

What is the biggest building?

The library. It has the most stories.

Which American had the biggest family?

George Washington, because he was the father of his country.

When the biggest elephant in the world fell into a 30-foot well, how did they get it out?

Wet.

What is as big as an elephant but doesn't weigh anything?

An elephant's shadow.

What is the best way to catch an elephant?

Act like a nut and he'll follow you anywhere.

What has a big mouth but doesn't say a word?

A river.

Who was the biggest thief in history?

Atlas, because he held up the whole world.

What is the best way to hold a bat?

By the wings.

How can you spell too much with two letters?

XS (excess).

When does a mouse weigh as much as an elephant?

When the scale is broken.

Who wears the smallest hat?

A narrow-minded person.

What word grows smaller when you add two letters to it?

Add 'er' to short and it becomes shorter.

What is a midget skunk called?

A shrunk skunk.

What is smaller than an ant's mouth?

An ant's dinner.

What is the distance between a stupid person's ears?

Next to nothing.

What is a small laugh in Indian language?

A Minnehaha.

What dog is 100 years old?

A sentry (century) dog.

What is the longest word in the English language?

'Smiles,' because there is a 'mile' between the first and last letters.

What is the longest shortest word?

Abbreviation.

What is the longest view in the world?

Down a road with telephone poles, because then you can see from pole to pole.

What kind of clothing wears the longest?

Underwear, because it is never worn out.

Why is the longest human nose on record only 11 inches long?

> *Because if it were 12 inches long it would be a foot.*

When is a miniskirt long?

> *When a midget wears it.*

What is the shortest month?

> *May. It has only three letters.*

What kind of pine has the sharpest needles?

> *Porcupine.*

What flower is happiest?

> *Gladiola.*

What is the hottest day of the week?

> *Friday (Fry day).*

What is the hottest part of a man's face?

> *His sideburns.*

What side of a fire is the hottest?

> *The fireside.*

When was beef at its highest?

> *When the cow jumped over the moon.*

What fish has the lowest voice?

A bass.

What person adds best in hot weather?

A summer.

What is the laziest mountain in the world?

Mt Everest.

What are the laziest animals on the farm?

Chickens. They are always laying (lying) around.

What is the poorest plant?

A vine, because it can't support itself.

What birds are noisiest?

Whooping cranes.

What person has the loudest voice?

The ice cream (I scream) man.

What is the cleverest animal?

A skunk, because it makes a lot of scents (sense).

Which is faster, hot or cold?

Hot, because you can catch cold.

8 Mad Mad Mad

How does a witch tell time?

With a witch watch.

Who drives away all of his customers?

A taxicab driver.

What driver doesn't have a licence?

A screw driver.

What do you call a high-priced barber's shop?

A clip joint.

If you cross a telephone and a pair of scissors, what do you get?

Snippy answers.

If you cross a telephone and a lobster what will you get?

Snappy talk.

Who is bigger, Mrs Bigger or her baby?

Her baby is a little Bigger.

What is purple and 5,000 miles long?

The Grape Wall of China.

What is green, has two legs and a trunk?

A seasick tourist.

What do you call an Indian woman who complains a lot?

A squaw-ker.

What kind of ears do trains have?

Engineers.

Why does a dog have fur?

If it didn't, it would be a little bear.

What game is played in the bathroom?

Ring around the tub.

Why shouldn't you tell secrets when a clock is around?

Because time will tell.

What is a drill team?

A group of dentists who work together.

What kind of tables do people eat?

Vegetables.

Where can you always find health, wealth and happiness?

In the dictionary.

What is an astronaut's favourite meal?

Launch.

What can you serve but never eat?

A tennis ball.

Why do we dress baby girls in pink and baby boys in blue?

Because they can't dress themselves.

What is the difference between an umbrella and a person who never stops talking?

The umbrella can be shut up.

Why do people buy things with their credit cards?

They get a charge out of it.

What is the most important use for cowhide?

It helps keep the cow together.

Who was the first to have a mobile home?

A turtle.

What is a wisecrack?

An educated hole in the wall.

A man who worked in the butcher's shop was 6 feet tall, had red hair and wore size 11 shoes. What did he weigh?

Meat.

What is lemonade?

When you help an old lemon cross the street.

What socks do you find in your back yard?

Garden hose.

What has a head, can't think, but drives?

A hammer.

What kind of test does a vampire take in school?

A blood test.

Where do young country dogs sleep?

In pup tents.

What is the best way to prevent milk from turning sour?

Leave it in the cow.

How does a coffee pot feel when it is hot?

Perky.

What is blue, green, yellow, purple, brown, black, and grey?

A box of crayons.

How can you make any watch a stopwatch?

Don't wind it.

What is a dog catcher?

A Spot remover.

What did the two vampires do from midnight to 12:10?

They took a coffin break.

How can you make money fast?

Glue it to the floor.

How can you make a soup rich?

> *Add 14 carrots (carats) to it.*

Why did the hippie put his money in the refrigerator?

> *He liked cold cash.*

What happened when the man asked the salesman for a good belt?

> *'O.K., you asked for it,' the salesman said as he gave him a good belt.*

How does a pair of pants feel when it is ironed?

> *Depressed.*

Why was the shoe unhappy?

> *Because his father was a loafer and his mother a sneaker.*

What did one skunk say to the other?

> *'So do you!'*

What did the fly say when he landed on the book?

> *'I think I read this story before.'*

What is 10 + 5 minus 15? What is 3 + 6 minus 9? What is 17 + 3 minus 20?

> *All that work for nothing!*

What do people in America call little black cats?

> *Kittens.*

How do you make a Venetian blind?

> *Stick a finger in his eye.*

What is the difference between twice twenty-two and twice two and twenty?

> *One is 44, the other is 24.*

If Washington's wife went to Washington while Washington's washwoman washed Washington's woollies, how many W's are there in all?

None. There are no W's in 'all'.

Where did the three little kittens find their mittens?

In the Yellow Pages.

9 Strange—But True

Why does a chicken lay an egg?

If she dropped it, it would break.

How can you drop an egg 3 feet without breaking it?

Drop it 4 feet. For the first 3 the egg will not hit anything.

Why is a room full of married couples empty?

Because there is not a single person in it.

What is the difference between a greedy person and an electric toaster?

One takes the most and the other makes the toast.

What man is strong enough to hold up a car with one hand?

A policeman.

Why do you always start to walk with the right foot first?

Because when you move one foot, the other one is always left-behind.

When do you swallow your words?

When you eat alphabet soup.

How can you be sure you have counterfeit money?

If it's a two-pound note, you can sure.

What goes out black and comes in white?

A black cow in a snowstorm.

Is it better to write on a full or on an empty stomach?

Neither. Paper is much better.

Where do fish wash themselves?

In the river basin.

What can you add to a bucket of water that will make it weigh less?

Holes.

Where do cars get the most flat tyres?

Where there is a fork in the road.

What kind of bird is always around when there is something to eat or drink?

A swallow.

What lands as often on its tail as it does its head?

A penny.

Why is the number nine like a peacock?

Because it is nothing without its tail.

Why don't scarecrows have any fun?

Because they are stuffed shirts.

How can you go without sleep for seven days and not be tired?

Sleep at night.

Why are identical twins like a broken alarm clock?

Because they are dead ringers.

What bus crossed the ocean?

Columbus.

What kind of tickle doesn't make you laugh?

A tickle in your throat.

How do you make a cigarette lighter?

Take out the tobacco.

How do you make notes of stone?

Rearrange the letters.

What kind of pool can't you swim in?

A car pool.

Why are dogs like trees?

They both have barks.

What kind of umbrella does the Queen of England carry on a rainy day?

A wet one.

What goes through a door but never goes in or out?

A keyhole.

What can turn without moving?

Milk. It can turn sour.

What code message is the same from left to right, right to left, upside down and right side up?

S O S.

How is a pig like a horse?

When a pig is hungry he eats like a horse, and when a horse is hungry he eats like a pig.

Why does the stork stand on one leg only?

If he lifted it, he would fall down.

On which side does a chicken have the most feathers?

On the outside.

Why do you say that whales talk a lot?

Because they are always spouting off.

What invention allows you to see through walls?

A window.

What has two legs like an Indian, two eyes like an Indian, two hands like an Indian, looks just like an Indian – but is not an Indian?

The picture of an Indian.

What is the difference between a banana and a bell?

You can only peel (peal) the banana once.

What can a whole apple do that half an apple can't do?

It can look round.

How many acorns grow on the average pine tree?

None. Pine trees don't have acorns.

What is always behind the times?

The back of a clock.

When is a man not a man?

When he turns into an alley.

What baby is born with whiskers?

A kitten.

How should you treat a baby goat?

Like a kid.

What kind of coat has no sleeves, no buttons, no pockets and won't keep you warm?

A coat of paint.

What kind of fall makes you unconscious but doesn't hurt you?

Falling asleep.

What turns everything around but doesn't move?

A mirror.

What was the largest island in the world before Australia was discovered?

Australia.

How do we know Rome was built at night?

Because Rome wasn't built in a day.

What lives in winter, dies in summer, and grows with its roots upwards?

An icicle.

Why do hummingbirds hum?
Because they can't read music.

What kind of pliers do you use in arithmetic?
Multipliers.

What has four fingers and a thumb but is not a hand?
A glove.

What is the hardest thing about learning to skate?
The ice.

What has a hundred limbs but can't walk?
A tree.

What is the longest word in the world?
Rubber, because it stretches.

When will a net hold water?
When the water is frozen into ice.

How much dirt is there in a hole exactly one foot deep and one foot across?

None. A hole is empty.

What is locomotion?

A crazy dance.

If you had 5 potatoes and had to divide them equally between 3 people, what should you do?

Mash them first.

What do they do with a tree after they chop it down?

Chop it up.

10 That's Entertainment

What is the easiest way to get on TV?

Sit on your set.

What happened to the kid who ran away with the circus?

The police made him bring it back.

Where did King Arthur go for entertainment?

To a nightclub (knight club).

What animals are poor dancers?

Four-legged ones, because they have two left feet.

Why couldn't anyone play cards on the ark?

Because Noah sat on the deck.

Why is a crossword puzzle like a quarrel?

Because one word leads to another.

What newspaper did the cavemen read?

The Prehistoric Times.

Where do snowflakes dance?

At the snowball.

Where do golfers dance?

At the golf ball.

Where do chickens dance?

At the fowl ball.

Where do butchers dance?
At the meatball.

What holiday does Dracula celebrate in November?
Fangsgiving (Thanksgiving).

What is a perfect name for a selfish girl?
Mimi (me, me).

What is a musical pickle?
A piccolo.

When do ghosts haunt skyscrapers?
When they are in high spirits.

Why did the owl make everyone laugh?
Because he was a howl.

Who has more fun when you tickle a mule?
He may enjoy it, but you'll get a bigger kick out of it.

Why are comedians like doctors?

Because they keep people in stitches.

Did you hear the story about the piece of butter?

Never mind. I don't want to spread it around.

What is the favourite ride of ghost children?

The roller ghoster (coaster).

Why can't an elephant ride a bicycle?

Because he doesn't have a thumb to ring the bell.

What fairground ride breaks up romances?

A merry-go-round. When the ride is over, people stop going around with each other.

What kind of book does Frankenstein like to read?

A novel with a cemetery plot.

Where is the best place to have a bubble gum contest?

On a choo-choo train.

What is a horse's favourite song?
  'Big Horse (because) I Love You.'

What is a ghost's favourite song?
  'A-Haunting We Will Go.'

What is a boiling kettle's favourite song?
  'Home on the Range.'

What keeps out flies and shows movies?
  Screens.

What is green and sings?
  Elvis Parsley.

Why are jazz musicians so sweet?
  Because they play in jam sessions.

What is a fund for needy musicians?
  A band aid.

What is in fashion but always out of date?
  The letter F.

Why is the circusman who was shot out of the cannon
not working anymore?
  Because he was discharged.

What kind of phone makes music?
  A saxophone.

What did one firecracker say to the other firecracker?
  'My pop is bigger than your pop.'

What fish is famous?
  A starfish.

Why are movie stars cool?

Because they have so many fans.

What is as round as the moon, as black as coal, and has a hole in the middle?

A gramophone record.

Why was the gramophone record nervous?

You would be too if you lived on spins and needles.

Why is a gramophone needle like a chicken?

They both scratch.

What famous dance music did Charles Dickens write?

'Oliver Twist.'

What dance do you do when summer is over?

Tango (tan go).

Why did the little kid dance on the jar of jam?

Because the top said, 'Twist to open.'

What do you call someone who hates operas?

An operator (opera-hater).

11 Riddles
for Thinkers

Why is the world like a faulty jigsaw puzzle?

Because a peace (piece) is missing.

What can be caught and heard but never seen?

A remark.

What can be measured but has no length, width or thickness?

The temperature.

What gets harder to catch the faster you run?

Your breath.

A frog fell into a well 12 feet deep. He could jump 3 feet, but every time he jumped 3 feet, he fell back 2 feet. How many times did he have to jump to get out of the well?

The tenth jump took him out. (On the tenth jump he reached 13 feet and was out.)

What is the difference between a dog and a gossip?

One has a wagging tail, the other a wagging tongue.

Why does a dog wag his tail?

Because no one else will wag it for him.

What is the best way to clean up a dirty mind?

Think a litter bit less.

How long should a person's legs be?

Long enough to reach the ground.

What gets wetter the more it dries?

A towel.

What has 6 legs, but walks with only 4?

A horse with a rider.

What didn't Adam and Eve have that everyone else in the world has had?

Parents.

Who invented the first aeroplane that didn't fly?

The Wrong Brothers.

When is a longhand quicker than shorthand?

On a clock.

Would you rather an elephant attacked you or a gorilla?

I'd rather he attacked the gorilla.

How does an elephant get down from a tree?

He sits on a leaf and waits for the fall.

When is your mind like a rumpled bed?

When it isn't made up yet.

On the way to a water hole a zebra met 6 giraffes. Each giraffe had 3 monkeys hanging from its neck. Each monkey had 2 birds on its tail. How many animals were going to the water hole?

Only the zebra. All the rest were coming back from the hole.

What did the sardine call the submarine?

A can with people in it.

How many legs does a mule have if you call its tail a leg?

Only four. Calling a tail a leg doesn't make it one.

What can you break with only one word?

Silence.

What has cities with no houses, rivers without water, and forests without trees?

A map.

What flies when it's on and floats when it's off?

A feather.

What has a big mouth but can't talk?

A jar.

Spell extra wise in two letters.

YY (2 y's)

Almost everyone needs it, asks for it, gives it, but almost nobody takes it. What is it?

Advice.

What is brought to the table and cut, but never eaten?

A deck of cards.

What question can you never answer 'yes' to?

'Are you asleep?'

Why is a poor friend better than a rich one?

Because a friend in need is a friend indeed.

Why is it interesting to study mummies?

Because you can get so wrapped up in them.

With what vegetable do you throw away the outside, cook the inside, eat the outside, and throw away the inside?

Corn on the cob.

What kind of tea helps you feel brave?

Safety.

Why do mother kangaroos hate rainy days?

Because then the children have to play inside.

How can you tell the difference between trees?

Listen to their barks.

What can't you see that is always before you?
The future.

What can you hold without your hands?
Your breath.

What can you give away and still keep?
A cold.

What comes from a tree and fights cavities?
A toothpick.

When is it correct to say, 'I is?'
'I is the letter after H.'

What word allows you to take two letters and get one?
Alone.

What is boiled then cooled, sweetened then soured?

Iced tea with lemon.

If 5 cats catch 5 mice in 5 minutes, how long will it take one cat to catch a mouse?

Five minutes.

The more you crack it, the more people like you. What is it?

A smile.

What is the beginning of eternity,
The end of time and space;
The beginning of every end,
And the end of every race?

The letter E.

Why do dogs scratch themselves?

Because they are the only ones who know where it itches.

12 What Do You Want To Be When You Grow Up?

What did the invisible girl want to be when she grew up?

> *A gone-gone dancer.*

What are doctors?

> *People who practise medicine but charge as if they know it.*

What kind of doctor treats ducks?

> *A quack.*

What is a thirsty physician?

> *A dry doc(k).*

What did the laundry man say to the impatient customer?

> *'Keep your shirt on!'*

What is the difference between a dressmaker and a farmer?

> *A dressmaker sews what she gathers, a farmer gathers what he sows.*

What is the difference between a jeweller and a gaoler?

A jeweller sells watches, a gaoler watches cells.

Why did the spy pull the sheets over his head?

He was an undercover agent.

Why do people dislike going to the dentist?

Because he is boring.

Why was the banker bored?

Because he had lost interest in everything.

What is the difference between a tailor and a horse trainer?

One mends a tear, the other tends a mare.

How do undertakers speak?

Gravely.

Why is a cobbler like a clergyman?

Both try to save soles (souls).

What do you call a minister named 'Fiddle?'

Fiddle, D.D.

What person tries to make you smile most of the time?

A photographer.

Why was the photographer arrested?

Because he shot people and blew them up.

What did Cinderella say when her photos didn't show up?

'Some day my prints (prince) will come.'

Why is a drama teacher like the Pony Express?

Because he is a stage coach.

What do atomic scientists do when they go on holiday?

They go fission (fishing).

How is a judge like an English teacher?

They both hand out long sentences.

What does a farmer grow if he works hard enough?
Tired.

Who makes a million pounds a day?
Someone who works in a mint.

Why are twin doctors puzzling?
They are a paradox (pair of docs).

What kind of artist can't you trust?
A sculptor because he is always chiselling.

Why shouldn't you believe painters?
Because they spread it on thick.

What did the painter say to the wall?
'One more crack like that and I'll plaster you!'

How do you learn to work in an ice cream parlour?
You go to sundae (Sunday) school.

Why did the lazy man want to work in the bakery?
Because he was a loafer.

Why did the baker stop making doughnuts?
Because he got tired of the whole (hole) thing.

Why did the baker stop baking bread?
Because he wasn't making enough dough.

Why did the baker quit his job?
Because his work was so crummy (crumby).

What did the woman say to the adding machine?
'I'm counting on you.'

Why was the cowboy a lot of laughs?
He was always horsing around.

What was Noah's profession?

He was an arkitect (architect).

What kind of a truck does a ballerina drive?

A toe (tow) truck.

What kind of car does an electrician drive?

A Volts Wagon (Volkswagen).

What is an astronomer?

A night watchman with a college education.

For what person do all men take off their hats?

The barber.

If you crossed a gangster and a dustbin man, what would you have?

Organized grime (crime).

Why are dustbin men unhappy?

Because they are down in the dumps so much.

If the Pilgrims came over on the *Mayflower*, how did the barbers arrive?

On clipper ships.

If you crossed a jeweller and a laundry man, what would you have?

Ring around the collar.

Why was Count Dracula glad to help young vampires?

He liked to see new blood in the business.

Why did the woman who mended bowls go crazy?

She was around cracked pots (crackpots) too long.

What kind of job did the lazy man get?

He stood around so long doing nothing, he became a dust collector.

Why did the girl who worked for the telephone company sing all the time?

Because she was an operetta (operator).

13 Trouble
Trouble Trouble

When things go wrong, what can you always count on?
Your fingers.

Why was the musician arrested?
He got into treble (trouble).

Why were screams coming from the kitchen?
The cook was beating the eggs.

Is it dangerous to swim on a full stomach?
Yes. It is better to swim in water.

Why is banana peel on the sidewalk like music?
Because if you don't C sharp you'll B flat.

If you plug your electric blanket into the toaster, what happens?
You pop up all night.

For how long a period of time did Cain hate his brother?
As long as he was Abel (able).

What happened when the man sat on a pin?
Nothing. It was a safety pin.

Why did the spy speak in a whisper?
Because he was on a hush-hush mission.

What should a girl wear when she wants to end a fight?

Makeup.

What kind of spy hangs around department stores?

A counterspy.

Why is an eye like a man being flogged?

Because it's under the lash.

What did the delicatessen sell after it burned down?

Smoked meats.

What three letters in the alphabet frighten criminals?

C.I.D.

What criminals can you find in a shoe store?

A pair of sneakers.

What diploma do criminals get?

The third degree.

When is a clock nervous?

When it is all wound up.

Why should a clock never be put upstairs?

It might run down and strike one.

Why do people beat their clocks?

To kill time.

A police officer had a brother, but the brother had no brother. How could this be?

The police officer was a woman.

Who were the first gamblers?

Adam and Eve. They had a paradise (pair of dice).

How can you avoid falling hair?

Get out of the way.

Why wasn't the girl afraid of the shark?

Because it was a man-eating shark.

Spell mousetrap with three letters.

C-A-T.

Why is a dictionary dangerous?

Because it has 'dynamite' in it.

A policeman saw a truck driver going the wrong way down a one-way street, but didn't give him a ticket. Why not?

The truck driver was walking.

Why did the dragon swallow the pesty knight?

Because he was a pill.

If you were walking in a jungle and saw a lion, what time would it be?

Time to run.

Why shouldn't you grab a tiger by his tail?

It may only be his tail, but it could be your end.

If an African lion fought an African tiger, who would win?

Neither. There are no tigers in Africa.

Why does a dog chasing a rabbit resemble a bald-headed man?

He makes a little hare (hair) go a long way.

What would you have if your car's motor was in flames?

A fire engine.

What did the rug say to the floor?

'I've got you covered.'

What did the picture say to the wall?

'I've been framed.'

What did the cork say to the bottle?

'If you don't behave yourself, I'll plug you.'

What did one cucumber say to the other cucumber?

'If you kept your big mouth shut, we wouldn't be in this pickle.'

Why did the hens refuse to lay any more eggs?

Because they were tired of working for chicken feed.

What would happen if black widow spiders were as big as horses?

If one bit you, you could ride it to the hospital.

What Indian goes to court?

A Sioux (sue) Indian.

What kind of suits do lawyers wear?

Lawsuits.

Where is the best place to hide a lawyer?

In a brief case.

When did the criminal get smart?

When the judge threw the book at him.

Why is your heart like a policeman?

Because it follows a regular beat.

Can you spell jealousy with two letters?

NV (envy).

What happens if an axe falls on your car?

You have an axe-i-dent (accident).

What kind of soldier doesn't need bullets?

A soldier who is always shooting his mouth off.

Why did the cowboy get a hot seat?

Because he rode the range.

When is an army totally destroyed?

When it is in quarters.

What is in the army and is nutty?

A colonel (kernel).

Why did the kid punch the bed?
His mother told him to hit the hay.

Why was the lobster arrested?
Because he was always pinching things.

Why did the sheriff arrest the tree?
Because its leaves rustled.

Why was the dirty kid arrested?
For grime (crime).

Why were the tennis players arrested?
Because they were involved with racquets (rackets).

14 Winners & Losers

How do chickens start a race?

From scratch.

What is a fast duck?

A quick quack.

Why did the orange stop in the middle of the road?

It ran out of juice.

A lemon and an orange were on a high diving board. The orange jumped off. Why didn't the lemon?

Because it was yellow.

Why did they throw the elephants out of the swimming pool?

Because they couldn't hold their trunks up.

If you were swimming in the ocean and a big alligator attacked you, what should you do?

Nothing. There are no alligators in the ocean.

Why shouldn't you tell a joke while you are ice skating?

Because the ice might crack up.

Why don't sheep have much money?

Because they're always getting fleeced.

Why did the kangaroo mother scold her child?

For eating biscuits in bed.

Why wasn't the elephant allowed on the aeroplane?

Because his trunk was too big to fit under the seat.

What kind of party do prisoners in jail like most of all?

A going-away party.

When do clocks die?

When their time is up.

What game can be dangerous to your mental health?

Marbles, if you lose them.

What stars go to jail?

Shooting stars.

What did the bee say to the rose?

'Hi Bud!'

What did the rose answer?

'Buzz off!'

What did the blackbird say to the scarecrow?

'I can beat the stuffing out of you!'

What did one grape say to the other grape?

'If it wasn't for you, we wouldn't be in this jam.'

Two hockey teams played a game. One team won but no man scored. How could that be?

Both were all-girl teams.

Why was Cinderella thrown off the netball team?

Because she ran away from the ball.

What team cries when it loses?

A bawl club.

What is the difference between an ice cream cone and a bully?

You lick one, the other licks you.

Two men were playing draughts. They played five games, and each man won the same number of games. How is that possible?

They played different people.

When it rains cats and dogs, what do you step into?

Poodles.

What did the frankfurter say when the dog bit him?

'It's a dog-eat-dog world.'

What line do children stand on to use the wading pool?

A wading (waiting) line.

How is a ghost child taught to count to ten?

One, boo, three, four, five, six, seven, hate, nine, frighten.

What did the yacht say to the dock?

'Yacht's (what's) up, Doc?'

What did the pitcher say to the cup?

'I'll have none of your lip.'

When is it bad luck to have a black cat follow you?

When you are a mouse.

What is a person who steals Honda bikes?

A Honda-taker (undertaker).

What do you get if your sheep studies karate?

A lamb chop.

What kind of skates wear out quickly?

Cheapskates (cheap skates).

How do fireflies start a race?

When somebody says, 'Ready, steady, glow!'

What is the best way to win a race?

Run faster than anybody else.

Why do you run faster when you have a cold?

You have a racing pulse and a running nose.

If George Washington were alive today, why couldn't he throw a silver dollar across the Potomac?

Because a dollar doesn't go as far as it used to.

What kind of sandwich speaks for itself?

A tongue sandwich.

Why is an airline pilot like a football player?

They both want to make safe touchdowns.

Who are the happiest people at the football game?

The cheerleaders.

What colour is a cheerleader?

Yeller (yellow).

If your watch is broken, why can't you go fishing?

Because you don't have the time.

What is the best way to communicate with a fish?

Drop him a line.

What did one fish say to the other?

'If you keep your big mouth shut, you won't get caught.'

What game do girls dislike?

Soccer (sock her).

What kind of dog hangs around bowling alleys?

A setter.

What famous prize do cats win?

The A-cat-emy (Academy) Award.

What dog has money?

A bloodhound, because he is always picking up scents (cents).

Why are dogs experts on trees?

They have to be if they don't want to bark up the wrong one.

If you're crazy about chess, why should you keep away from squirrels?

Because squirrels eat chestnuts (chess nuts).

15 Oh, No!

What would you call two bananas?
A pair of slippers.

What would you call the life story of a car?
An autobiography.

What do you call a hippie's wife?
Mississippi (Mrs Hippie).

What part of a clock is always old?
The second hand.

What do you get if you cross a squirrel and a kangaroo?
An animal that carries nuts in its pocket.

What is a banged-up uscd car?
A car in first-crash condition.

What does Santa Claus do when it is not Christmas?
He is probably a farmer because he always says, 'Hoe, hoe, hoe!'

Why is a book like a king?
Because they both have pages.

What is black and white and red all over?
A newspaper.

What is black and white and red all over?
A sunburned zebra.

What is black and white and red all over?

A skunk with nappy rash.

What is black and white and red all over?

A blushing penguin.

What is the correct height for people to stand?

Over two feet.

What does a dog get when it graduates from dog school?

A pedigree.

What is the difference between a dog and a flea?

A dog can have fleas but a flea can't have dogs.

What kind of truck is always a 'he' and never a 'she'?

A mail truck.

Why are men going bald at an older age these days?

Because they're wearing their hair longer.

Who invented the telephone?

The Phoenicians (phone-itions).

What are the most faithful insects?

Ticks. Once they find friends, they stick to them.

What would happen if you swallowed your knife and fork?

You would have to eat with your hands.

If a papa bull eats three bales of hay and a baby bull eats one bale, how much hay will a mama bull eat?

Nothing. There is no such thing as a mama bull.

Where can you always find diamonds?

In a pack of cards.

Why do statues and paintings of George Washington always show him standing?

Because he would never lie.

What causes baldness?

Lack of hair.

What happened when Frankenstein met a girl monster?

They fell in love at first fright.

What animals are well educated?

Fish, because they go around in schools.

What is an ocean?

Where buoy meets gull (boy meets girl).

What is green and pecks on trees?

Woody Wood Pickle.

What is a parasite?

Something you see in Paris.

What did the boy Frankenstein say to the girl Frankenstein?

'You are so electrocute.'

How can you tell if a ghost is about to faint?

He gets pale as a sheet.

What did one invisible man say to the other invisible man?

'It's nice to see you again.'

What do you call someone who carries a dictionary in his jeans?

Smarty pants.

When is an army like a salesman making out a bill?

When it is ready to charge.

Why did the three little pigs leave home?

Because their father was a big boar (bore).

Why did the girl sit on her watch?

She wanted to be on time.

What 8-letter word has one letter in it?

Envelope.

What are the three swiftest means of communication?

Telephone, telegraph and tell-a-secret.

Why do cats sleep better in summer than in winter?

> *Because summer brings the caterpillar (cat a pillow).*

What is an ultimate?

> *The last person you marry.*

'Did you hear the story about the smog?'

> *'You don't have to tell me, it's all over town.'*

What is big and purple and lies in the sea?

> *Grape Britain.*

What is a ship for good writers?

> *Penmanship.*

What is the front part of a geography book?

> *The table of continents (contents).*

What did one car say to the other?

> *'You look familiar. Haven't we bumped into each other before?'*

What two words have thousands of letters in them?

> *Post office.*

When do princes become kings?

> *Mostly in April, when the rains (reigns) begin.*

Why do hurricanes have girl's names?

If they were named after boys, they would have to be called 'himmicanes.'

If fish lived on land, where would they live?

In Finland.

If two's company and three's a crowd, what is four and five?

Nine.

16 Far Out

What do you do with a green monster?
Wait till he ripens.

What sits on the bottom of the sea and shakes?
A nervous wreck.

What is a witch doctor's mistake?
A voodoo boo-boo.

What kind of jokes did Einstein make?
Wisecracks.

At what time of day was Adam born?
A little before Eve.

What is long and yellow and always points north?
A magnetic banana.

Why did the athlete blink his eyelashes all day?
He needed batting practice.

What did the little kid do with the dead battery?
He buried it.

What occurs once in every minute, twice in every moment, but not once in a thousand years?
The letter M.

What are the six main seasons?
Summer, autumn, winter, spring, salt and pepper.

What is a locomotive?

A crazy reason for doing something.

Where does a liar sleep?

In a bunk bed.

Which astronaut wears the biggest helmet?

The one with the biggest head.

What does an astronaut do when he gets angry?

He blasts off.

What do people do in a clock factory?

They make faces all day.

What do you call a person who looks over your shoulder while you are eating at the lunch counter?

A counterspy.

What is purple and conquered the world?

Alexander the Grape.

What travels around the world but stays in a corner?

A stamp.

What do you have if you cross a witch and a millionaire?

A witch (rich) person.

What would you get if you crossed a skunk and an eagle?

An animal that stunk to high heaven.

How can you make varnish disappear?

Take out the R.

Is a unicorn male or female?

Female. The unicorn is a myth (Miss).

What time is it when a knight looks at his belly button?

It is the middle of the night (knight).

Why did the horses go on strike?

To get more horsepower.

Why did the cowboy's car stop?

It had Injun (engine) trouble.

What did the explorer say when he saw the Pacific Ocean for the first time?

'Long time no see (sea).'

Are you crazy if you talk to yourself?

Not unless you answer.

What is the difference between a counterfeit pound note and a crazy rabbit?

One is bad money, the other is a mad bunny.

What is the difference between a cloud and a spanked child?

One pours down rain, the other roars with pain.

What would you get if you crossed a pigeon, a frog, and a prehistoric monster?

A pigeon-toed (toad) dinosaur.

What do you get when you cross a lion and a parrot?

I don't know, but if it wants a biscuit, you'd better give it one.

In what school do you have to drop out in order to graduate?

Parachute school.

If you cross a lion and a monkey, what do you have?

A swinging lion.

If you cross a camera and a mirror, what do you get?

A camera that takes pictures of itself.

What do you get if you cross a jumbo jet and a kangaroo?

A plane that makes short hops.

Why did it take three husky Boy Scouts to help the little old lady cross the street?

Because she didn't want to go.

What do you call an ocean plantation?

A pharmacy (farm-asea).

What holds the moon up?

Moonbeams.

Why is a grape religious?

Because it comes from divine (the vine).

Where do good pigs go when they die?

To a sty in the sky.

What did one angel say to the other angel?

'Halo.'

What kind of clothes did Cinderella wear?

Wish and wear clothes.

Why does the Statue of Liberty stand?

Because she can't sit down.

If a millionaire sits on his gold, who sits on silver?

The Lone Ranger.

Why did the pirate put a chicken where he buried his treasure?

Because eggs (X) marks the spot.

Why did the one-eyed chicken cross the road?

Because there was a Bird's Eye factory across the street.

Why did the chicken cross the road twice?

Because she was a double-crosser.

Why did the chicken go just halfway across the road?

She wanted to lay it on the line.

Why did the chicken cross the road?

With traffic the way it is today, probably to commit suicide.

What happened to Humpty Dumpty after he had a great fall?

He was made into an egg salad sandwich for all the king's men.

Why did Humpty Dumpty have a great fall?

To make up for a bad summer.

What would you have if a young goat fell into a blender?

A mixed-up kid.

Why doesn't Saint Nicholas shave?

Every time he tries, he nicks himself.

What kind of salad do hippies like?

Tossed salads because they are all shook up.

How many balls of string would it take to reach the moon?

One, if it were long enough.

Why won't people ever go to the moon for their holidays?

Because it lacks atmosphere.

What kind of insects live on the moon?

Lunatics (lunar ticks).

Why are false teeth like stars?

Because they come out at night.

What person watches the stars?

A movie fan.

What did the stamp say to the envelope?

'I've become attached to you.'

What did the envelope say to the stamp?

'Stick with me and we'll go places.'

17 Weird Characters

Why did the musician strike the gramophone record with a hammer?

He wanted a hit record.

What did the woodchopper do when he didn't know the time?

He axed (asked) someone.

If a girl ate her mother and father, what would that make her?

An orphan.

What is Frankenstein's favourite waterway?

The Erie (eerie) Canal.

Why did the dog run around in circles?

Because he was a watchdog and wanted to wind himself up.

Why was the puppy fat?

Because he always had a second yelping (helping).

What did the vegetable say when it was wrapped for another day?

'Curses, foiled again!'

What did Sir Lancelot wear to bed?

A nightgown (knight gown).

Why do elephants paint their toenails red?

So that they can hide in the strawberry patch.

What does a two-hundred-pound mouse say?

'Here, Kitty, Kitty.'

Why do elephants wear green nail polish?

So they can hide in the pea patch.

Where does Frankenstein's wife have her hair done?

At the ugly parlour.

Who was the first swinger?

Tarzan.

What is green and flies?

Super Pickle.

Why does Batman brush his teeth at least three times a day?

To prevent bat (bad) breath.

Why did the hippie paint the landscape?

Because he wanted to make the scene.

If you cross a pig and a young goat, what do you get?

A dirty kid.

What do you get if you cross a porcupine and a young goat?

A stuck-up kid.

What gives milk and says, 'Oom, oom'?

A cow walking backwards.

What kind of boats do vampires take when they travel?

Blood vessels.

Why did the rabbit wear a shower cap?

Because he didn't want his hare (hair) to get wet.

Why did the kid roll rocks down the hill?

He wanted to see the Rolling Stones.

What kind of crew does a monster ship have?

A skeleton crew.

Why did the farmer feed his cow money?

He wanted rich milk.

What branch of the army do babies join?

The infantry.

What would you call a knight caught in a windstorm?

A nightingale (knight in gale).

Why did the pig act up?

Because he was a big ham.

Chief Running Water had two sons. What were their names?

Hot and Cold.

Why did the astronomer hit himself on the head in the afternoon?

He wanted to see stars during the day.

What was Batman doing in the tree?

Looking for Robin's nest.

Why did the elephant swallow a camphor ball?

To keep moths out of his trunk.

Why did the nasty kid put ice cubes in his aunt's bed?

Because he wanted to make antifreeze.

Why did the potato farmer use a steam roller?

Because he wanted to grow mashed potatoes.

Why did the mad chef watch the lazy cow?

He liked to see the meat loaf.

Why did the secretary ask for a round envelope?

Because she wanted to mail a circular.

Why didn't Count Dracula get married?

Because he was a bat-chelor (bachelor)

Why did the girl aim a cannon at the peas?

Because her mother told her to shell them.

What animal eats and drinks with its tail?

All do. No animal takes off its tail when eating and drinking.

Why do you get a charge out of reading the newspaper?

Because it is full of current events.

18 Don't Look at These!

What do you call Eskimo cows?

Eskimoos.

What do you get if you cross a centipede and a parrot?

A walkie-talkie.

What do you get if you cross a chick and a guitar?

A chicken that makes music when you pluck it.

What do you get if you cross a homing pigeon and a woodpecker?

A bird that not only delivers messages, but also knocks on the door.

What do you get if you cross a cocker spaniel, a poodle and a rooster?

A cockapoodledoo.

What do you get if you cross a canary and a tiger?

I don't know, but when it sings you'd better listen.

What do two oceans say when they meet?

They don't say anything, they just wave.

What nationality is Santa Claus?

North Polish.

What is long and thin and goes, 'Hith, Hith'?

A snake with a lisp.

If a buttercup is yellow, what colour is a hiccup?

Burple.

What do you call it when pigs do their laundry?

Hogwash!

What do liars do after they die?

Lie still.

If you crossed King Kong and a bell, what would you have?

A ding-dong King Kong.

How do you know that carrots are good for the eyes?

Have you ever seen a rabbit wearing spectacles?

What did the cannibal have for lunch?

Baked beings (beans).

Why should you stay calm when you meet a cannibal?

You don't want to get into a stew.

What goes, 'Clomp, clomp, clomp, squish. Clomp, clomp, clomp, squish?'

An elephant with a wet sneaker.

Why did the boy's mother knit him three socks for Christmas?

Because he grew another foot.

What did George Washington say to his men before crossing the Delaware by boat?

'Get in!'

Why was George Washington buried at Mount Vernon?

Because he was dead.

What would you get if Minnehaha married Santa Claus?

Minnehaha hoho.

Where was the Magna Carta signed?

At the bottom.

What do you call a knife that cuts four loaves of bread at the same time?

A four-loaf cleaver (clover).

What is white outside, green inside, and hops?

A frog sandwich.

What is a ghoul's favourite food?

Goulash.

What wears a black cape, flies through the night, and bites?

A mosquito in a black cape.

What is a twip?

A twip is what a wabbit takes when he wides a twain.

Why shouldn't you sweep out a room?

The job is too big. Just sweep out the dirt and leave the room there.

Who invented spaghetti?

Someone who used his noodle.

Where do old Volkswagens go?

To the old Volks (folks) home.

What is green and dangerous?

A thundering herd of pickles.

Why do dragons sleep during the day?

So that they can fight knights (nights).

What is yellow, smooth and very dangerous?

Shark-infested custard.

What part of a car causes the most accidents?

The nut behind the wheel.

Why would someone in gaol want to catch the measles?

So he could break out.

How do you keep a rhinoceros from charging?

Take away his credit cards.

Why is a grouchy kindergarten teacher like a collection of old car parts?

She's a crank surrounded by a bunch of little nuts.

What is a fast tricycle?

A tot rod.

What is the best way to hunt bear?

With your clothes off.

What does a mummy child call its parents?

Mummy and Deady.

How do mummies behave?

In a grave manner.

What is on a ghost's bicycle wheels?

Spooks (spokes).

What is a haunted wigwam?

A creepy teepee.

Why did the ghost kid measure himself against the wall?

Because he wanted to know if he gruesome (grew some).

19 Super Stumpers

Why did the little biscuit cry?

Because its mother was a wafer (away for) a long time.

Who was the first person to swear?

Eve. When Adam asked if he could kiss her, she said, 'I don't care Adam if you do.'

Why does Tarzan yell?

He is so strong that every time he beats his chest, it hurts.

When can you throw a watch out of the window, go down three flights of stairs, and catch it?

When it is 10 minutes slow.

What 5-letter word has 6 left when you take 2 letters away?

Sixty.

What is black when it is clean and white when it is dirty?

A blackboard.

If two wrongs don't make a right, what did two rights make?

An aeroplane.

What is the best way to make time race?

Use the spur of the moment.

Why was the bride unhappy with the first cake she baked?

Because her husband took it for granite (granted).

What is an angel in heaven?

A blessing in disguise (the skies).

What is long and slippery and whistles 'Dixie' backwards?

General Robert E. Eel.

What kind of cars come from Norway?

Norwegian fiords (Fords).

What comes in different flavours, shakes a lot and lives in the ocean?

A jellyfish.

What can a bird do that a man cannot do?

Take a bath in a saucer.

Why did the hippie go to the North Pole?

To see the other cool people.

What is the difference between a horse and the weather?

One is reined up, the other rains down.

What do you call someone whose library books are overdue?

A bookkeeper.

What instrument lets you see monsters?

A horror-scope.

Why can't you read a stupid person's mind?
The type is too small.

What do you call someone who helps on a farm?
A pharmacist (farm assist).

What did the skunk say when the wind changed?
'It all comes back to me now.'

What did the shy pebble say?
'I wish I were a little bolder (boulder).'

What are the last three hairs on a dog's tail called?
Dog hairs.

How do trees become petrified?
The wind makes them rock.

Why is a turkey more evil than a chicken?
Because a turkey is always a'gobblin' (goblin).

Why was the geometry teacher boring?
Because he was a square and talked in circles.

What do you get if you stand too close to the fireplace?

Hearth (heart) burn.

Why is it that when you tear down a building it is the same thing as when you build a building?

Because when you build a building you 'raise' it; when you tear down a building, you still 'raze' it.

Why wouldn't the kid study history?

Because he thought it better to let bygones be bygones.

How do you get two pints of milk into a one-pint bottle?

Condense it.

If you crossed an axe and a stick, what would you get?

A chopstick.

What is mind?

No matter.

What is matter?

Never mind.

On what day of the year did soldiers start wars in history?

March fourth.

What is the difference between a man parking his car and a man smashing dishes?

One sets the brakes, the other breaks the sets.

What is a dieter's motto?

'If at first you don't recede, diet again.'

Why was the United Nations worried when the waiter dropped a platter of turkey on the floor?

It meant the fall of Turkey, the ruin of Greece, and the break-up of China.

What is black, shiny, lives in trees and is very dangerous?

A crow with a machine gun.

What is too much for one, enough for two, but nothing for three?

A secret.

Which is better – happiness or a penny?

A penny. Nothing is better than happiness – and a penny is better than nothing.

When does eleven plus two equal one?

On a watch face.

If all the letters of the alphabet were invited to a tea party, what letters would be late?

The letters U, V, W, X, Y, Z. They all come after T (tea).

On a warm day a man bought two fishes. When he reached home, he had three. How could this be?

He still had two fishes – and one smelt.

A man drove all the way from London to Edinburgh without knowing he had a flat tyre. How is that possible?

It was his spare tyre that was flat.

Once upon a time there was a king. Set before him were three glasses. Two of them were filled with water. The other one was empty. What was the king's name?

Philip (fill up) the Third.

How are the deaths of a sculptor and a barber different?

One makes faces and busts; the other curls up and dyes (dies).

Why couldn't Batman go fishing?

Because Robin ate all the worms.

If you add a father, a mother and a baby, what do you get?

Two and one to carry.

What is rhubarb?

Celery with high blood pressure.

If you see a counterfeit pound note lying in the street, should you leave it or pick it up?

> *Better pick it up. You might get arrested for passing it.*

ENID BLYTON is Dragon's bestselling author. Her books have sold millions of copies throughout the world and have delighted children of many nations. Here is a list of her books available in Dragon Books:

FIRST TERM AT MALORY TOWERS	50p	☐
SECOND TERM AT MALORY TOWERS	50p	☐
THIRD YEAR AT MALORY TOWERS	50p	☐
UPPER FOURTH AT MALORY TOWERS	50p	☐
IN THE FIFTH AT MALORY TOWERS	50p	☐
LAST TERM AT MALORY TOWERS	50p	☐
MALORY TOWERS GIFT SET	£2·55	☐

6 Books by Enid Blyton

THE TWINS AT ST CLARE'S	50p	☐
SUMMER TERM AT ST CLARE'S	50p	☐
SECOND FORM AT ST CLARE'S	50p	☐
CLAUDINE AT ST CLARE'S	50p	☐
FIFTH FORMERS AT ST CLARE'S	50p	☐
THE O'SULLIVAN TWINS	50p	☐
ST CLARE'S GIFT SET	£2·55	☐

5 Books by Enid Blyton

MYSTERY OF THE BANSHEE TOWERS	50p	☐
MYSTERY OF THE BURNT COTTAGE	50p	☐
MYSTERY OF THE DISAPPEARING CAT	40p	☐
MYSTERY OF THE HIDDEN HOUSE	50p	☐
MYSTERY OF HOLLY LANE	50p	☐
MYSTERY OF THE INVISIBLE THIEF	50p	☐
MYSTERY OF THE MISSING MAN	40p	☐
MYSTERY OF THE MISSING NECKLACE	50p	☐
MYSTERY OF THE PANTOMIME CAT	50p	☐
MYSTERY OF THE SECRET ROOM	50p	☐
MYSTERY OF THE SPITEFUL LETTERS	40p	☐
MYSTERY OF THE STRANGE BUNDLE	50p	☐
MYSTERY OF THE STRANGE MESSAGES	50p	☐
MYSTERY OF TALLY-HO COTTAGE	50p	☐
MYSTERY OF THE VANISHED PRINCE	40p	☐

CHILDREN'S LIFE OF CHRIST	30p	☐
THE BOY WHO TURNED INTO AN ENGINE	40p	☐
THE BOOK OF NAUGHTY CHILDREN	35p	☐
A SECOND BOOK OF NAUGHTY CHILDREN	35p	☐

PONY BOOKS are very popular with boys and girls.
Dragon Books have a fine selection by the best authors to choose from:

JUMP TO THE STARS	Gillian Baxter	50p	☐
THE DIFFICULT SUMMER	Gillian Baxter	50p	☐
THE PERFECT HORSE	Gillian Baxter	50p	☐
SUE'S CIRCUS HORSE	Judith Berrisford	50p	☐
PONIES ALL SUMMER	Judith Berrisford	50p	☐
THE FOREST ADVENTURE	Judith Berrisford	50p	☐
TROUBLE AT PONYWAYS	Judith Berrisford	50p	☐
SILVER BRUMBY'S KINGDOM	Elyne Mitchell	50p	☐
SILVER BRUMBIES OF THE SOUTH	Elyne Mitchell	50p	☐
SILVER BRUMBY	Elyne Mitchell	35p	☐
SILVER BRUMBY'S DAUGHTER	Elyne Mitchell	40p	☐
SILVER BRUMBY WHIRLWIND	Elyne Mitchell	35p	☐
MOON FILLY	Elyne Mitchell	50p	☐
MY FRIEND FLICKA PART 1	Mary O'Hara	60p	☐
MY FRIEND FLICKA PART 2	Mary O'Hara	40p	☐
GREEN GRASS OF WYOMING 1	Mary O'Hara	40p	☐
GREEN GRASS OF WYOMING 2	Mary O'Hara	40p	☐
GREEN GRASS OF WYOMING 3	Mary O'Hara	40p	☐
THUNDERHEAD 1	Mary O'Hara	40p	☐
THUNDERHEAD 2	Mary O'Hara	40p	☐
THUNDERHEAD 3	Mary O'Hara	40p	☐
FOR WANT OF A SADDLE	Christine Pullein-Thompson	50p	☐
IMPOSSIBLE HORSE	Christine Pullein-Thompson	35p	☐
THE SECOND MOUNT	Christine Pullein-Thompson	35p	☐
THE EMPTY FIELD	Christine Pullein-Thompson	50p	☐
THREE TO RIDE	Christine Pullein-Thompson	35p	☐
THE PONY DOPERS	Christine Pullein-Thompson	50p	☐
PONY PATROL	Christine Pullein-Thompson	40p	☐
PONY PATROL S.O.S.	Christine Pullein-Thompson	40p	☐
PONY PATROL FIGHTS BACK	Christine Pullein-Thompson	50p	☐
FIRST ROSETTE	Christine Pullein-Thompson	35p	☐
THE LOST PONY	Christine Pullein-Thompson	50p	☐

A great selection of puzzle books from Dragon.

FIGURE IT OUT 1	50p ☐
FIGURE IT OUT 2	50p ☐

Two Books by Michael Holt

Two crackling collections of computational conundrums ranging from the stupendously simple to the fiendishly difficult.

PICTURE WORDS	50p ☐
WORD HUNT	50p ☐
IN OTHER WORDS	50p ☐
MY WORD	50p ☐
WORD FOR WORD	50p ☐
WHAT'S THE WORD	50p ☐

Six Books by Ronald Ridout

Six word-puzzle books from a master with words. They begin easily but by the time you've puzzled out the last puzzle in the last book you'll be a real word expert yourself.

FIRST PUZZLES	50p ☐
KONKY PUZZLES	50p ☐
ACTIVE PUZZLES	50p ☐
PUZZLES GALORE	50p ☐
MORE PUZZLES	50p ☐
TOP PUZZLES	50p ☐

Six Books by Ronald Ridout

Just about the widest range of puzzles ever published in paperback. Work from *First Puzzles* to *Top Puzzles* and you'll really be a Puzzle Champion.

Outstanding fiction from the Dragon List.

INVISIBLE MAGIC   Elisabeth Beresford 60p ☐

What happens when a modern boy *half*-releases a centuries old spell.

DANGEROUS MAGIC   Elisabeth Beresford 60p ☐

Sammy and Eleanor pledge themselves to help the Unicorn get back to its own Place and Time. But where is that? And when?

THE BIG TEST   Roy Brown 50p ☐

A fast-moving adventure story set in the streets around London's Oval cricket ground on the last day of the Test.

A NAG CALLED WEDNESDAY   Roy Brown 50p ☐

When Liz and Larry 'find' a horse wandering the London streets, they think that keeping it will be easy. A funny and exciting chase story.

ROBIN HOOD   Antonia Fraser 40p ☐

The adventures of the fabulous hero in a stirring retelling.

NO PONIES FOR MISS POBJOY

          Ursula Moray Williams 50p ☐
The girls of Canterdown were mad on horses. Their new headmistress cared only for cars – and for passing exams. A hilarious school story with a difference.

THE HOUSE IN CORNWALL   Noel Streatfeild 35p ☐

A west country holiday with an unknown uncle could be fun. Or it could be dismal. Edward, Sorrell and Wish certainly were to find it surprising – and dangerous.

THE WINTER OF ENCHANTMENT

          Victoria Walker 20p ☐
A magic mirror transports Sebastian from his Victorian world of winter snow to the magic world of Melissa, Mantari and the wicked enchanter.

Fun and information from the Dragon non-fiction list.

FREE FUN   Eve Barwell   65p ☐

A great collection of ideas for things to do, indoors and out, on your own or with a friend. And they all cost absolutely nothing.

EXPERIMENTS WITH EVERYDAY OBJECTS
                          Kevin Goldstein-Jackson   65p ☐

Nearly one hundred fascinating experiments to carry out with the minimum of (mostly) household equipment. A swift raid on the kitchen should supply all you'll need for hours of fun.

STRANGE TO RELATE   Melvin Harris   60p ☐

A startling collection of strange but true stories – and the even stranger things people have been fooled into believing.

THE DRAGON SEASIDE BOOK   Deborah Manley   50p ☐

What to do at the seaside when it's raining, when the tide's out or when you're just bored with sandcastles and swimming.

All these books are available at your local bookshop or newsagent, or can be ordered direct from the publisher. Just tick the titles you want and fill in the form below.

Name ....

Address ....

....

Write to Dragon Cash Sales, PO Box 11, Falmouth, Cornwall TR10 9EN.

Please enclose remittance to the value of the cover price plus:

UK: 22p for the first book plus 10p per copy for each additional book ordered to a maximum charge of 82p.

BFPO and EIRE: 22p for the first book plus 10p per copy for the next 6 books, thereafter 3p per book.

OVERSEAS: 30p for the first book and 10p for each additional book.

Granada Publishing reserve the right to show new retail prices on covers, which may differ from those previously advertised in the text or elsewhere.